THE HEROINE

OF THE

TITANIC

A TALE BOTH TRUE
AND OTHERWISE OF THE
LIFE OF MOLLY BROWN

JOAN W. BLOS

ILLUSTRATED BY

TENNESSEE DIXON

Morrow Junior Books / New York

To Joanne & George, Marsha & Cy

J.W.B.

To my mother and father,
Elizabeth and Noah

T.D.

Watercolors and ink were used for the full-color art. The text type is 14 pt. Clearface.

Text copyright © 1991 by Joan W. Blos
Illustrations copyright © 1991 by Tennessee Dixon
All rights reserved. No part of this book may be reproduced or utilized
in any form or by any means, electronic or mechanical,
including photocopying, recording
or by any information storage and retrieval system,
without permission in writing from the Publisher.
Inquiries should be addressed to
William Morrow and Company, Inc.,
1350 Avenue of the Americas,
New York, NY 10019.
Printed in Hong Kong by South China Printing Company (1988) Ltd.
1 2 3 4 5 6 7 8 9 10
Library of Congress Cataloging-in-Publication Data
Blos, Joan W.
The heroine of the Titanic : a tale both true and
otherwise of the life of Molly Brown / Joan W. Blos ; illustrated by
Tennessee Dixon.
p.   cm.
Summary: Anecdotal account of some of the adventurous activities of
Molly Brown, with an emphasis on her survival of the sinking of the Titanic.
ISBN 0-688-07546-0.—ISBN 0-688-07547-9 (lib. bdg.)
1. Brown, Margaret Tobin, 1867-1932—Juvenile literature.
2. Titanic (Steamship)—Juvenile literature.   3. United States—
Biography—Juvenile literature.   [1. Brown, Margaret Tobin,
1867-1932.   2. Titanic (Steamship)   3. United States—Biography.
4. Voyages and travels.]   I. Dixon, Tennessee, ill.   II. Title.
CT275.B7656B56   1991
973.91'092—dc20
[B]
[92]   90-35369   CIP   AC

Molly Brown?
You asking for Molly Brown?
Born in Hannibal, Missouri,
On the poorer side of town,
She grew up and went to Leadville
And married J.J. Brown.
And when the ship *Titanic* sank,
Molly did not go down.

July 18, 1867

The night was dark and stormy.
Close by the town of Hannibal, Missouri,
the waters of the Mississippi River
rolled like mountains between their banks
and crashed upon the shore.

In a white frame house
set back from Deckler Alley,
a red-haired baby girl was born
to John and Johanna Tobin.
They named the baby Margaret,
and she was their second child.

How she came to be Molly later on
is anybody's guess.
There are some who say it goes to show
that she was just too slippery
for so much as a name to stick.

Molly was her mother's pride and joy
and her father's favorite.
Often and again he would tell his little daughter
of the night that she was born.

"A regular cyclone howled outside . . ."
"But Daddy, there *are* no cyclones in Missouri!"
"Hush, child, I said a cyclone.
For it's true as a hammer and a ten-penny nail,
it was no common storm that blew
the night that you were born!"

Much as she loved the stories that he told,
she loved his sweet songs even more.
She listened when he sang them
till she knew them all by heart.

Molly had two half sisters,
two brothers, and one sister.
Her older sisters taught her to be good.
"Answer when you're spoken to," they said.
"Help when others are in need,
and learn all you can at school."
Her brothers taught her, too.
They taught her to spit straight,
whistle in tune,
and win when she played at marbles.

1886

Just before Molly turned nineteen,
she read in the local newspaper
of men getting rich mining silver
in a place called Colorado.
She got out her old school atlas
and looked it up.
Colorado was west of the prairie
and crossed by the Rocky Mountains.
"I'll go there directly," Molly said.
"I've a mind to be rich, too."

Quick as she could, she packed up her possessions,
waved her family good-bye,
and when the next train, westbound, left the depot,
Molly was on board.

What were you thinking of then, Molly Brown,
Leaving behind you all you had known?
As the fields full of wheat
Stood up tall in the heat,
As the train
Crossed the plain
Going clickety-clack,
Did you know you would never go back?

Leadville, Colorado

Leadville was a tough town then,
bigger but not much fancier
than an ordinary mining camp.
By one count it had "ninety-seven saloons,
along with twenty-three restaurants,
fifty-four boarding houses,
two sausage makers,
one soap manufacturer,
and countless gambling halls."
There was also an opera house.
Leadville's wooden sidewalks were taken up each night
and filled, by day, with miners
who had come there to get rich.

They talked of nothing but silver.
Some of them quickly struck it rich,
but most of them did not.
In Leadville there were misery and trouble
as well as overnight success
and pockets full of cash.

Molly had not been there long
when the manager of a concert hall
happened to hear her sing.

The manager hired her on the spot,
and from her first performance on,
the miners went wild over Molly.
They whistled and cheered when she came out onstage.
They climbed up on their seats.
Often they threw down gold or silver coins
by way of appreciation.

Molly Brown? Molly Brown?
As a duck will take to water
And a princess to a crown,
So Molly took to Leadville
And to James Joseph Brown.

Later That Same Summer

J.J. was quite a bit older than Molly;
good-looking, fast-talking, and smart.
He started in courting right away
and was kind and polite to Molly.
They went on picnics and buggy rides
high on the mountain slopes.

Up there, where the mountain flowers grew,
the air was so pure and thin and bright,
it could make a person dizzy
just breathing in that air.

"Jim," said Molly, as they finished up a lunch
of sandwiches and strong cheese,
"you ought to've been at the theater—
two, three nights ago.
It was then," she said, "the boys got carried away
and threw down so much gold as well as silver,
they had to get a snowplow in
to clear away the drifts."

Jim sat up smartly to listen,
full of respect and love.
But when her eyes began to shine,
and she couldn't help but laugh,
he chased her down the mountainside
for telling such a fib.

Once, while strolling arm in arm,
Molly told Jim about life back in Missouri
when she was growing up:
how poor they had been; the fun they had had;
how she wanted to be sure that her daddy,
when he grew old,
would never be in need.
"There're three things I'm set on in this life," she said.
"Having fun,
        doing good,
                being sure there's plenty of money."
"I'll do what I can," J.J. promised.

Soon after that they got married,
and Molly became Mrs. Brown.

One house they had was near Jim's mine,
up on Iron Hill.
Larry was the first child born to them;
after that there came Helen.
Molly kept the children neat and clean
and also looked after the house.

Sometimes, when the wind blew in
and the temperature dropped below zero,
Molly would gather the children close
and warm them with her stories
of when she was a little girl.
"Once," she'd begin, "I was swimming in the river,
and I swam so fast and dove so deep,
I got stuck in the mud at the bottom.

"It took two donkeys, pulling two days straight,
to get me out of that.
Then, when they had raised me to the top,
I was covered all over with Mississippi mud,
right up to my neck.
Matter of fact, I looked so like a statue
that if my daddy hadn't come along just then,
they'd have probably put me in the park
as a roost for homeless pigeons."
"Oh, Ma," they said, "they wouldn't have never done it."
"Oh, they *would*," she said. But she smiled.

By this time, J.J. was making so much money,
they set silver dollars in the bedroom floor
just for decoration.
And when Molly's parents came to Leadville for a visit,
Molly bought presents for everyone—
a filigreed pin for her ma to wear,
and slippers for her daddy.
Every night she warmed those slippers by the fire;
and after her daddy put them on,
he'd sit back and take his ease
like a proper gentleman.

Molly Brown? You mean Mrs. J.J. Brown?
When she and *Mr.* J.J. Brown
Decided to move to Denver town,
They bought the kids a horse and cart
And filled the house with works of art;
Got four stone lions to guard the door
And a bearskin rug for the parquet floor.
So anyone passing by could tell
That the J.J. Browns were doing well.

1894

The new house had modern conveniences
such as indoor plumbing and electric lights.
Also, it was large and grand,
and fashionably located near the capitol building.

One night J.J. got the two of them mixed up
and banged on the doors of the capitol,
thinking it was home.
He wished it had never happened.
Molly, on the other hand, told everyone they knew!
She thought that it made a good story,
and she liked being talked about.

"It means you're important," she explained,
"and I'll see to it that they keep talking."
In this she was true to her word.

1903

Denver was bright and lively.
There were parties nearly every night;
opera singers came to entertain
and authors to give lectures.
Whatever the rich and famous did,
Polly Pry, a newspaper reporter,
told of it in the paper
that was published the next day.

Now Polly Pry and Molly Brown
had never gotten along.
Each took every chance she got
to make the other look foolish.
So when Molly Brown wrote Polly Pry a letter,
and the letter was full of highfalutin language
and low-down spelling errors,
Polly Pry had it printed in the paper
just the way it was.

Next morning, all over Denver,
people laughed at Molly
and said she was putting on airs.
"So they think I need more learning," Molly fumed.
"Well, it will be my pleasure
to show them a thing or two."

Molly, *Molly*, MOLLY Brown
Bought herself a brand-new gown.
Out she went and down she fell
(With an *S* and a *P* and an *E, L, L*).
Too hurt to laugh, too big to cry—
The cause of it all? Miss Polly Pry.

1909

The years in between had not been happy ones.
J.J. had tired of Molly's commotions
and gone back to Leadville to live.
Larry and Helen had been sent to boarding school.
The house seemed empty and old.
No use staying here, thought Molly.
I always liked to travel.
Now I can see the world.

Wherever Molly went she made new friends
and was generous, cheerful, and kind.
She saw all the sights of Europe
and was proud to study French.
Narrowly missing a memorable monsoon,
she traveled east to China and Tibet.
The trip was a great success.

"Dear Larry and Helen," she wrote,
"Every day I am becoming more of a lady.
In Honolulu, I learned to play the ukulele.
In Siam, I mastered the native dances.
And, in Switzerland, I learned how to yodel.
I will be coming home soon.
Love, Mrs. J.J. Brown."

The ship Molly chose was the R.M.S. *Titanic*,
said to be unsinkable
and the fastest ship afloat.
It was to be the great ship's maiden voyage,
and a gala crossing was planned.

April 15, 1912

On the fourth night out of Southampton,
the *Titanic* rammed an iceberg.
Molly grabbed a fur coat
and hurried up on deck.

It was clear that the ship was sinking.
Worse, there were too few lifeboats
to save all the people on board.
"Women and children first!" the Captain ordered.
So Molly was placed in lifeboat #6
with twenty-six other passengers
and a member of the crew.

"We will all be lost!" the terrified sailor shouted.
"Move over, sailor," Molly shouted back.
"I was born in a cyclone on the Mississippi River,
and I don't plan on drowning at sea."

All through the night, till a rescue ship arrived,
Molly kept up her spirits
and encouraged the others as well.

"There's fixes tighter than this one," she declared.
"Why once when I was but a child,
I swam so fast and dove so deep,
I got stuck in the mud of the Mississippi River,
right up to my neck.
It took *three* donkeys, pulling *three* days straight,
to get me out of that.
And if my daddy hadn't come along just then,
there's no telling what would have happened."

Then, to make sure they got the joke,
she put back her head and yodeled.
"I learned that in Switzerland," she said,
seeing their surprise.

But Molly did more than tell stories.
She rowed until her hands were sore,
and made sure that the others took turns.
She spread out her coat as a blanket,
and she never gave up hope.

As soon as the rescue ship reached shore,
people came to meet it
and to see if they could help.
Several friends brought clothes and a hat for Molly.
Reporters gathered quickly, eager for the news.

"EXTRA!" shouted the newsboys.
"EXTRA! Read all about it!"
"'Denver's Mrs. J.J. Brown Helps Many to Survive.'"

The New York Times

CARPATHIA HERE TO-NIGHT WITH TITANIC'S SURVIVORS;
HER REPORTS SHOW 700 SAVED; 1500 GONE TO DEATH;
WIRELESS MESSAGE OUTLINES THE TRAGIC STORY

Molly Brown? The unsinkable Molly Brown?
There was glory in her story,
And it won her great renown.
For when the ship *Titanic* sank,
Molly did not go down.

Twenty Years Later: 1932

Molly had had what she wanted out of life:
had fun, been rich, done good.
Now she was living at the Barbizon Hotel
in the middle of New York City.
Her room was full of souvenirs—
things she had gathered to help her to remember
all she had been and done.

First there were the days when she was a little girl,
Johnny Tobin's daughter.
She hummed his songs, the ones that she liked best,
not bothering with the words.

She told herself the stories
that Larry and Helen had loved.
I swam so fast and dove so deep, she remembered,
it took FOUR donkeys pulling FOUR days straight . . .
She thought of the days in Leadville
when J.J. had loved her so dearly
and Larry and Helen were young.
"Those were the happy days," she said,
"the ones that are good to remember."

But now in Leadville, times were hard.
No one was buying silver
and the wind from the mountains was cold.

Leadville needs you, Molly Brown.
Her mines are shut down tight.
And Leadville's children fear that they
Will have no gifts on Christmas Day,
No carols Christmas night.

Molly quickly determined to lend a helping hand.
She would make sure that Leadville had a tree—
the biggest one in the county,
the biggest one ever seen!
Its branches would be hung
with packages gaily wrapped,
each one filled with warm new clothes,
enough for all the children.

At R. H. Macy's and Klein's-on-the-Square,
she bought dozens of pairs of socks and gloves,
half a hundred sweaters, and as many knitted caps.
She had them sent to Leadville, parcel post,
and planned to follow soon.

It didn't work out that way.
Molly Brown died in October, and the tree was never set up.

At Christmas, though, her nephew traveled to Leadville
and gave out all the presents.
And just as Molly had known it would,
the wind blew in from the mountains
and the temperature dropped below zero.
Then the children put on their bright new clothes—
the caps, the socks, the sweaters—
and they hardly noticed the cold.

"That Molly Brown," they heard their parents say.
"She always did have a way with her
and a heart that was as big as a ham."
The children weren't sure exactly what that meant,
but they thought it was probably good.

MOLLY BROWN · LOVED by ALL · 1867–1932

Molly Brown? Molly Brown?
We'll remember you forever,
Molly Brown.
Your words and actions bold,
Unlike silver, unlike gold,
Endure, Molly Brown.
You live on!

Author's Note

Surprisingly little has been written of Molly-Margaret-Maggie-Tobin-Brown. There is no trace of her in any of the standard biographical dictionaries or usual reference works.

"Was she real?" a young librarian asked, frustrated by our search.

Molly Brown was real, all right! As Mrs. J.J. Brown, she is praised in newspaper articles that appeared nationwide at the time of the *Titanic's* sinking, and her name can be seen on the list of its passengers (ominously) and on that of the survivors (happily). The *National Geographic Magazine* of December 1986 makes brief mention of her in its article on the exploration by robot of the newly located underwater wreck. The Molly Brown House Museum in Denver, Colorado, offers several brief publications. For the rest, one is dependent on primary source materials available to the researcher and pertinent bits of information scattered through books on the Southwest, on mining, on Denver. (The musical *The Unsinkable Molly Brown* and the film based on it have made Molly Brown's name pleasantly familiar. But, like this book, both go beyond known facts.) Under the circumstances, and because Molly Brown was something of a confabulator herself, especially as she got older, my subtitle might more rigorously have stated: "Her Life Not So Much As It Was Lived but As She Might Have Liked It Known."

The best thing to do, if you want to know more about Molly, is to travel, as I did, to Denver. There you can visit the house where Molly lived and hear more Molly stories.

Acknowledgments

Thanks are due to Roberta Hagood, of Hannibal, Missouri, for early help in obtaining information; to Lyn Spenst, of Littleton, Colorado, and Christine Whitacre, of Denver, for being so very generous, for encouragement and assistance at the time of my visit. The guides at the Molly Brown House Museum were gracious and well-informed. I feel privileged to have had original materials made available to me at the House itself and in the historical collections of the Denver Public Library. Several curators at the Henry Ford Museum in Dearborn, Michigan, checked last-minute details. Finally, I wish to note that the quoted description of Leadville is taken from *Colorado Ghost Towns and Mining Camps* by Sandra Dallas, published by the University of Oklahoma Press in 1985.

—— J.W.B.

921   Blos, Joan W
Bro
        The heroine of the
        Titanic